I0701090

10 Pillars of Personal Growth

Realizing Your Potential
and Accepting Change

By

Israel Daniel

Disclaimer

By Israel Daniel, copyright ©
2024. All rights reserved. This
ebook's content is intended solely
for informative and educational
purposes. It is not meant to serve
as a replacement for expert
financial guidance. This ebook's
publishers and writers are not
financial counselors; thus, the
information inside should not be
interpreted as individual financial
advice. Before making any

financial decisions or putting any of the methods covered in this ebook into practice, readers are strongly advised to speak with licensed financial advisors. Any harm or injury arising from reliance on the information supplied herein is disclaimed by the writers and publishers.

Table of contents

Introduction

Starting a personal development journey is like going out on an unknown ocean with limitless opportunities and life-changing events. The desire to become the best version of oneself and realize one's full potential is what drives this journey, which starts with one step. In this introduction, we will examine the importance of personal growth, including the reasons why it is so important for people to go on this journey and the significant effects it may have on many facets of life.

In addition, we will lay the groundwork for the ten personal development pillars that will guide us on this journey of self-discovery. The quest for contentment and self-

actualization is at the core of
personal development. It is the
unrelenting pursuit of realizing
our potential, facing our
anxieties, and overcoming the
obstacles that have prevented us
from moving forward.
Every person's path is different,
influenced by their values, goals,
and experiences. The goal,
however, is still the same despite
the variety of routes taken: a life
full of meaning, passion, and
purpose.
Why is it vital to grow
personally? In other words, it
holds the secret to realizing our
full potential and leading an
abundant life. When we make a
commitment to our own
development, we let in fresh
perspectives, possibilities, and
challenges that help us grow and
reach new heights. Through
growth, we learn, develop, and,
in the end, become the people we
want to be. However, setting out
on a path of self-improvement is
not without its difficulties. It
takes bravery to face our
weaknesses, resiliency to get past
obstacles, and commitment to

keep going when things get tough. However, because they force us to venture outside of our comfort zones and embrace the unknown, it is precisely because of these obstacles that we grow the most.

It's critical to keep in mind that personal development is a lifetime process rather than a destination as we embark on this adventure together. It is a dedication to ongoing development and introspection, driven by a love of learning and self-belief. Although there may be times when we succeed and times when we struggle along the journey, every step we take will get us one step closer to being the best version of ourselves.

The ten pillars of personal growth that will guide us on our path will be examined throughout this book. Each pillar—self-awareness, goal-setting, resilience, and empowerment, for example—represents a key component of personal development that will support us as we meet the possibilities and difficulties that lie ahead. Together, let's set out on our voyage, eager to embrace the adventure that lies ahead and with open minds and hearts. We discover not just who we are but also who we can become when we pursue personal growth.

Pillar 1: Self-Awareness: Recognizing Your Inner World

The cornerstone of personal development and the base upon which all other pillars are built is self-awareness. It is the capacity to honestly and clearly reflect on our feelings, ideas, and actions in order to develop an understanding of who we really are. This chapter takes us on a voyage of self-discovery, exploring the depths of our minds to learn about the nuances of our inner environment.

The practice of mindfulness, which is the skill of being totally present in the moment without judgment or attachment, is a prerequisite for developing true self-awareness.

By practicing mindfulness, we may watch our thoughts and feelings as they come to us without becoming consumed by them. By practicing mindfulness, we can become more conscious of our inner workings and become aware of patterns and tendencies that we may not have previously recognized.

However, being self-aware involves more than just observation; it also necessitates being willing to face the difficult realities that are hidden from view. It entails accepting our weaknesses, owning up to our errors, and admitting our defects. We can only start the process of healing and development by shedding light on the deepest recesses of our psyche. Understanding our values, beliefs, and motivations—the principles that influence our decisions and behaviors—is another aspect of being self-aware.

We may live with more honesty and integrity if we make sure that our behaviors are consistent with our basic ideals. We can make deliberate decisions that are in line with our genuine selves thanks to this self-awareness, which gives us a greater sense of purpose and joy in life.

Journaling is an effective method for developing self-awareness. We can obtain important insights into our inner world by writing down our thoughts and feelings. By keeping a journal, we may monitor our development, spot trends, and examine our feelings in a secure and accepting environment.

Writing can help us discover fresh viewpoints and hidden truths, which can result in significant personal development. Knowing our talents and shortcomings is a crucial component of self-awareness.

Acknowledging our distinct aptitudes and skills allows us to utilize them to accomplish our objectives and surmount obstacles. Similarly, by being aware of our shortcomings, we may proactively work on becoming better and evolving. Greater success and fulfillment can be attained by using our strengths while actively addressing our areas for improvement when we are self-aware.

However, developing self-awareness is a lifetime process of inquiry and learning rather than a static state. Our self-awareness will expand as we mature and change, revealing new levels of awareness.

We can develop a stronger sense of self-awareness and lead more fulfilling lives by engaging in this ongoing process of introspection and reflection. Self-awareness is the cornerstone of personal development. We can better comprehend who we are and reach our full potential by developing a mindfulness practice, accepting our vulnerabilities, defining our values, and realizing our strengths and shortcomings.

By developing self-awareness, we can set out on a path of self-discovery that will increase our sense of authenticity, purpose, and fulfillment.

Pillar 2: Goal-Setting: Creating a Successful Route

Setting goals acts as the compass on our personal growth path, pointing us in the direction of our destination. It is the process of identifying our goals, turning them into doable tasks, and deciding to go for our desires. This chapter delves into the ways that goal-setting can change a person's life and the methods for creating a successful route. Setting goals is essentially about having a clear vision for the future and acting purposefully to make it a reality. Regardless of how big or small, immediate or long-term, our objectives provide us with focus and direction, inspiring us to push outside our comfort zones and pursue excellence.

Clearly defining our goals and our definition of success is the first step in creating goals. This entails evaluating our priorities, values, and interests in order to pinpoint the areas of our lives in which we wish to bring about constructive change.

We may make sure that our efforts are concentrated on the things that are really important to us by establishing goals that are consistent with our beliefs and aspirations. The next stage is to divide our goals into smaller, more doable tasks after we have identified them.

We may develop a roadmap for accomplishing our goals by using this chunking approach, which breaks things down into manageable actions that we can take one at a time. By dividing our objectives into more manageable benchmarks, we can keep up our pace and more accurately monitor our development.

Another crucial component of successful goal setting is creating SMART goals, or specific, measurable, achievable, relevant, and time-bound objectives. By giving us a precise framework for setting goals and monitoring our advancement, SMART goals

help to make sure that our efforts
are targeted and well-thought
out.

  We may improve our odds of
success and save ourselves from
being overwhelmed or
demoralized by creating SMART
goals. Setting objectives,
however, is merely the first step;
persistence, discipline, and
dedication are needed to see
them through.

  We are likely to run into
roadblocks and setbacks that
could perhaps stop us in our
tracks. We can, however,
overcome these obstacles and
keep advancing toward our goals
by keeping an optimistic outlook
and remaining committed to our
mission.

  Sharing our goals with others is
a great way to stay accountable
and motivated. We may establish
a network of accountability that
helps us stay on track and
motivates us to stick with our
goals by asking friends, family,
or mentors for help. Publicly
expressing our objectives can
also keep us energized and
motivated as we work to meet

the expectations of others who have faith in us. Maintaining our goals' efficacy and relevance requires us to examine and modify them frequently.

Our circumstances and priorities may change as we move forward on our personal growth journey; therefore, we will need to modify our goals accordingly. Our efforts will always be in line with our changing goals if we periodically review our goals and make the necessary corrections. Setting goals is a great way to direct our course toward achievement and reach our greatest potential.

We may make a road map for reaching our goals by defining them clearly, breaking them down into manageable steps, and making a commitment to pursuing them.

We may overcome challenges and maintain focus on our goals by using SMART goal-setting, accountability, and resilience. This will ultimately lead to increased achievement, fulfillment, and personal development.

Pillar 3: Adaptability: Succeeding Despite Misfortune

Resilience is the capacity to overcome obstacles, adjust to change, and recover from setbacks. It is a crucial ability on the path to personal development since it helps us get over obstacles and come out stronger and more resilient than before. This chapter delves into the transforming potential of resilience and the methods we may use to develop this essential trait in our lives.

There are many ups and downs, detours and unforeseen obstacles in life that put our fortitude and resilience to the test. Adversity can take many different forms, from professional setbacks to personal losses and disappointments, and it can leave us feeling helpless and demoralized.

Resilience, on the other hand, enables us to face life's challenges head-on with courage and grace, coming out of them stronger and more resilient than before. The capacity to keep a positive outlook in the face of difficulty is one of resilience's fundamental traits.

Resilient people look for chances for growth and solutions rather than focusing on the bad parts of a situation. They remain hopeful and upbeat even in the most dire circumstances because they see failures as transient impediments rather than insurmountable ones. The capacity to accept ambiguity and adjust to change is a crucial component of resilience. Because life is unpredictable, unforeseen circumstances have the power to derail us and undermine our sense of security.

On the other hand, resilient people can roll with the punches and welcome change as a chance for personal development. They continue to be adaptable and receptive, eager to consider novel ideas and embrace the unknown. Creating a solid support system of friends, family, and mentors who can offer support, direction, and perspective during trying times is another important aspect of building resilience.

We may draw strength from their presence and more easily weather life's storms when we surround ourselves with people who believe in us and support us when we need it most.

Building resilience also requires self-care and placing a high priority on our mental, emotional, and physical health. A vital component of self-care is finding time to relax and rejuvenate, participating in joyful and fulfilling activities, and asking for help when necessary. These actions help us become more resilient and adept at overcoming obstacles in life. Reframing our ideas and perceptions of hardship is a potent strategy for developing resilience. People who are resilient view setbacks as opportunities for growth and learning rather than as failures.

They welcome obstacles as opportunities to grow as people, acquire new abilities, and fortify their character. Adversity can be a chance for us to grow and transform ourselves if we change the way we think about it and embrace a growth-oriented viewpoint.

Self-compassion exercises and treating oneself with kindness and empathy when facing adversity are other aspects of cultivating resilience. Resilient people treat themselves with the same kindness and encouragement they would give to a friend in need, rather than being harsh and judgmental of themselves.

Without passing judgment, they accept their emotions and experiences and give themselves permission to mourn, heal, and go on at their own speed. On the path to personal development, resilience is a crucial ability that allows us to flourish in the face of difficulty and come out stronger and more resilient than before.

Reframing our ideas about adversity, practicing self-compassion, prioritizing self-care, accepting change, keeping an optimistic outlook, and practicing self-compassion are all ways that we can grow resilience in our lives and face life's obstacles with courage and grace. Resilience enables us to not only weather life's storms but also to grow and learn from them, which eventually results in increased success, happiness, and personal development.

Pillar 4: Mindfulness: Fostering Peace and Presence

Cultivating mindfulness has become more crucial than ever in our fast-paced, constantly-demanding, and distracted environment. The practice of mindfulness involves developing a profound awareness and acceptance of our thoughts, feelings, and experiences while remaining completely present in the moment without passing judgment or feeling any attachment. This chapter delves into the methods for developing presence and tranquility in our lives, as well as the transformational potential of mindfulness.

Fundamentally, mindfulness is about being open, curious, and accepting of the current moment while paying attention to it. It is the practice encounter.

Developing a nonjudgmental mindset toward our ideas and experiences is another aspect of mindfulness. Rather than categorizing our ideas as good or evil, right or wrong, we just notice them with compassion and curiosity, accepting them as they come to us without allowing them to control us.

By practicing this nonjudgmental awareness, we can break free from the hold of self-criticism and negative self-talk and develop an inner sense of acceptance and serenity.

Learning to develop an attitude of gratitude and appreciation for the present moment is another crucial component of mindfulness.

It is easy to take for granted the small pleasures and benefits that we are surrounded by every day in our hectic lives. But by engaging in mindfulness practices, we can learn to appreciate the beauty of the here and now and find contentment in life's little miracles, like a warm cup of tea, a soft wind, or a loved one's smile.

We can focus on the plenty in our lives rather than the things that are lacking by developing an attitude of thankfulness, which will increase our pleasure and sense of fulfillment. A further component of mindfulness is developing kindness and compassion for oneself and other people. It is easy to get sucked into the chase of achievement and success in our fast-paced, cutthroat society, frequently at the expense of our own and other people's wellbeing.

On the other hand, by engaging in mindfulness practices, we can develop empathy and compassion for both ourselves and other people, realizing our connection and common humanity. We may leave a more peaceful and compassionate world for ourselves and future generations if we treat ourselves and others with love and understanding.

The practice of meditation is one effective way to develop mindfulness. Sitting still and watching one's breath, thoughts, and feelings as they come up is the practice of meditation. We may train our minds to become more present-focused, peaceful, and focused through consistent meditation practice, which will increase our level of tranquility and clarity in day-to-day living. Mindful movement exercises like yoga, tai chi, or qigong are also good ways to develop awareness. These age-old techniques integrate meditation, breath awareness, and moderate exercise to help us develop mindfulness while also

enhancing our physical health
and general wellbeing.
We can become more in tune
with our body and the present
moment by moving consciously,
which promotes increased vigor
and serenity. Through the
practice of mindfulness, we may
effectively cultivate presence and
calm in our lives, which leads to
increased clarity, insight, and
fulfillment.
We can have more peace and
happiness in our lives by learning
to still our minds, developing a
nonjudgmental mindset,
exercising compassion and
kindness toward ourselves and
others, and developing gratitude
and appreciation. We may live
more present-minded,
purposeful, and peaceful lives by
practicing mindfulness and
learning to appreciate the beauty
of the moment as it is.
Emotional intelligence is a pillar
of the personal growth journey,
providing a technique to
gracefully negotiate the complex
web of interpersonal
connections. In this examination
of the 10 pillars of personal

growth, we get deeply into the essence of emotional intelligence and its significant influence on our interpersonal relationships.

1. **Awareness of Oneself: The Basis**

The foundation of emotional intelligence is self-awareness. It entails being aware of one's own feelings, advantages, disadvantages, and effects on other people. People can better understand their emotional triggers and behavioral patterns by developing self-awareness, which pave the way for the development of wholesome relationships.

2. **Self-Control: Understanding Emotional Reactions**

Self-regulation enables people to efficiently control their emotions, particularly in trying circumstances. It entails using self-control, avoiding rash decisions, and constructively expressing feelings. Self-control helps people build resilience, steer clear of pointless arguments, and create happy relationships.

3. **Empathy: Perceiving Things from Their Point of View**

One of the core components of emotional intelligence is empathy, or the capacity to comprehend and experience another person's emotions. People can build trust in their relationships and establish a stronger connection by putting themselves in other people's shoes. Empathy develops empathy, facilitates successful communication, and creates a sense of community.

4. **Active Listening: The Skill of Perception**

Active listening entails thoroughly interacting with

people in order to understand their message and feelings, in addition to simply hearing what they have to say. Active listening helps people establish rapport, validate the experiences of others, and foster deep connections. It fortifies the bonds between people and promotes respect for one another.

5. Communication: Overcoming Disparities

Building strong relationships requires effective communication. It includes expressing ideas, sentiments, and intentions with precision, sincerity, and authenticity. By developing their communication skills, people can reduce miscommunication, find constructive solutions to problems, and foster closeness and trust in their relationships.

6. Resolving Conflicts: Using Chances to Create Opportunities

Any relationship will inevitably have conflict, but how it is handled can have a big impact. Emotional intelligence fosters empathy, active listening, and open communication, which gives people the skills they need to resolve issues amicably. Resolving conflicts helps people grow, make their relationships stronger, and comprehend one another better.

7. Limitations: Respecting Oneself and Others

Having healthy relationships requires setting and upholding limits. People with emotional intelligence are able to recognize their needs, values, and boundaries and respectfully and assertively state them. Respecting boundaries helps people maintain their independence, foster respect for one another, and avoid relationship burnout or resentment.

8. **Adaptability: Accepting Shift**

The capacity to flexibly adapt to changing conditions and obstacles is known as adaptability. Through encouraging resilience, optimism, and a growth mindset, emotional intelligence facilitates adaptability. When people are flexible in their relationships, they can easily handle changes, accept one another's differences, and promote each other's development.

9. **Forgiveness: Heart Liberation**

Being able to forgive releases people from their resentment, rage, and bitterness. It is a transformational act. Through the development of empathy, perspective-taking, and emotional management, emotional intelligence promotes forgiveness. People can develop compassion, reestablish trust, and strengthen bonds in relationships by letting go of grudges and past injuries.

10. Gratitude: Cultivating Recognition

Practicing gratitude involves recognizing and being grateful for all of life's blessings. Gratitude is nurtured by emotional intelligence through the development of positivity, empathy, and mindfulness. In interpersonal interactions, expressing gratitude improves bonds, encourages appreciation for one another, and deepens the bond between people.

In summary When it comes to helping people grow personally, emotional intelligence is a beacon of light that enables them to navigate relationships with grace, empathy, and sincerity. People may create meaningful connections, settle disputes amicably, and build a happy existence full of harmonious relationships by developing self-awareness, emotional control, and empathy. Led by the insight of emotional intelligence, let us set out on a path of self-discovery and harmonious relationships as we embrace the 10 pillars of personal growth.

Pillar 5: Emotional Intelligence: Handling Relationships with Grace

Emotional intelligence, which is frequently considered the foundation of a healthy relationship, has the capacity to change exchanges into deep bonds infused with grace, compassion, and empathy. Within the broad field of human dynamics, becoming skilled at the fine art of gracefully managing relationships is like tending a garden of blossoming connections, where every encounter becomes a chance for development and mutual enrichment.

In its most basic form, emotional intelligence refers to a broad range of abilities that allow people to effectively sense, comprehend, and regulate their own emotions as well as those of others. It acts as a compass, directing us through the maze-like exchanges between people in which words alone frequently fail to fully express the breadth of our intentions and sentiments. Emotional intelligence is demonstrated in relationships through the capacity for genuine, compassionate communication, heartfelt listening, and empathy for the experiences of others. It's the skill of gracefully and resiliently dealing with the ups and downs of feelings, creating a climate of mutual respect and trust.

The development of self-awareness is essential to the practice of emotional intelligence since it serves as the foundation for all other practices. We may better understand how we behave in relationships and how we affect people around us by developing a deeper grasp of our own emotions, triggers, and behavioral patterns.

The basis for growing empathy—the capacity to put oneself in another person's shoes and perceive the world from their perspective—is this self-awareness. Meaningful connections are rooted in empathy, which enables us to create ties of solidarity and understanding with others. It makes it possible for us to identify and affirm the feelings of the people we engage with, fostering a secure environment in which they can express themselves freely and honestly. By showing others that we are genuinely able to see and hear them, we cultivate a feeling of acceptance and belonging. Emotional intelligence is like a lighthouse in the face of conflict and disagreement, pointing the way toward peace and understanding. It gives us the ability to handle challenging talks with poise and empathy, looking for points of agreement and understanding even when we disagree. Instead of becoming defensive or aggressive in the face of conflict, we can foster growth and a closer sense of connection when we approach it with curiosity and an open mind. In the end, developing emotional intelligence is a lifetime endeavor that calls for perseverance, introspection, and a commitment to development. By developing our capacity for graceful relationship navigation, we weave a rich web of connections that improve both our own and other people's lives. Genuine connection is becoming less and less common in our culture; emotional intelligence shines a light on the way to greater comprehension, empathy, and compassion.

Pillar 6: Lifelong Learning: Broadening Your Views

The process of picking up new information, abilities, and perspectives as one goes through life is called continuous learning. It holds the secret to happiness, career advancement, and personal development. In this investigation, we examine the importance of continual learning, its advantages, and methods for broadening perspectives and embracing lifetime learning.

1. **The importance of ongoing education**

The need for ongoing learning is more important than ever in the world we live in today, which is changing so quickly. People must constantly adapt and develop in response to changing society standards, industry changes, and technological breakthroughs. Constant learning helps people become more resilient, agile, and adaptable so they can take advantage of new possibilities and prosper in changing situations.

2. Advantages of Lifelong Learning

There are numerous advantages to continuous learning, both personally and professionally. It improves cognitive function, expands horizons, and piques intellectual interest. Furthermore, it increases self-efficacy, confidence, and self-esteem as people learn new abilities and conquer obstacles. Continuous learning promotes innovation and creativity, boosts employability, and offers avenues for career growth in the workplace.

3. Adopting a Growth Perspective

Continuous learning is based on a growth mindset, which is the conviction that skills can be acquired with commitment and work. Adopting a growth mindset enables people to rise to difficulties, persevere through setbacks, and see failures as chances for improvement. People who adopt a growth mindset realize their full potential and accept lifelong learning as a path toward self-improvement and self-discovery.

4. **Establishing learning objectives**

Establishing attainable learning objectives is crucial for directing and inspiring ongoing learning initiatives. Setting and achieving goals gives people a sense of purpose, direction, and focus as they advance in their learning. Whether learning a new language, gaining technical proficiency, or pursuing personal interests, defining learning objectives helps people monitor their progress and recognize achievements along the way.

5. Changing Up the Way You Teach

The spice of lifelong learning is variety. Reading, attending seminars, taking online courses, and getting hands-on experience are examples of diverse learning approaches that improve knowledge retention, comprehension, and application. People can enhance their learning potential and accommodate their specific learning preferences by experimenting with various learning methods.

6. Developing Inquiry

The spark that lights the flames of constant learning is curiosity. It encourages people to inquire, look for solutions, and investigate novel notions. Embracing the unfamiliar, questioning presumptions, and

keeping an open mind are all part of developing curiosity.
Fostering curiosity sets people on a path of exploration and sparks their enthusiasm for knowledge and creativity.

7. Accepting Failure as a Chance to Learn

An essential component of learning is failure. Rather than being afraid of failing, people can accept it as an important teaching moment. Resilience and growth are promoted through reviewing setbacks, noting lessons, and modifying plans of action in light of those insights. Reframing failure as a necessary step toward success helps people overcome obstacles with grace and tenacity.

8. Requesting mentorship and input

Mentorship and feedback are two very useful tools for lifelong learning. Asking for advice from mentors, colleagues, or specialists offers insightful comments, areas for growth, and constructive criticism. Furthermore, mentorship provides direction, assistance, and inspiration as learners traverse their educational path and surmount obstacles by utilizing the knowledge and insight of seasoned role models.

9. **Reflection and Integration Exercises**

The link that connects application and learning is reflection. People are better able to internalize knowledge and apply it to their lives when they take the time to reflect on their experiences, insights, and lessons gained. Through introspection, people broaden their awareness, acquire clarity, and pinpoint areas in which they still have room to improve.

10. **Giving Back: Disseminating Information**

People who learn new things on a constant basis have an obligation to share what they learn with others in order to return the favor. Sharing knowledge improves learning for both the provider and the recipient, whether via coaching, instructing, or participating in joint initiatives. Promoting a culture of information exchange allows people to improve the growth and progress of the group as a whole.

In summary The foundation of both professional and personal development is continuous learning, which helps people broaden their perspectives, embrace change, and prosper in a world that is always changing. People can set off on a lifelong learning journey that is full of growth, fulfillment, and discovery by adopting a growth mindset, setting goals, experimenting with different learning styles, and encouraging curiosity. As we make lifelong learning a priority, let's take advantage of the chance to broaden our perspectives, reach our full potential, and create a better future for present and future generations.

Pillar 7: Gratitude: Discovering Happiness in Ordinary Moments

Practicing gratitude has the capacity to change our lives and foster a deep sense of contentment and happiness. In this investigation of thankfulness, we look at its importance, advantages, and doable methods for using the practice of gratitude to discover delight in ordinary circumstances.

1. **Recognizing the Influence of Thankfulness**

Gratitude is an attitude and way of looking at life that goes beyond just saying "thank you." Fundamentally, being grateful means recognizing and appreciating all of life's blessings, no matter how great or small. Gratitude creates a sense of plenty, satisfaction, and joy by refocusing our attention from what we lack to what we have.

2. The Advantages of Appreciation

There are numerous advantages to practicing appreciation for one's physical, mental, and emotional health. According to research, gratitude improves resilience, fortifies relationships, and fosters general happiness and life satisfaction. Furthermore, thankfulness training improves mental and emotional health by lowering stress, increasing optimism, and cultivating a positive outlook.

3. **Developing an Appreciative Heart**

Mindfulness and purpose are the first steps in the transforming process of developing a grateful heart. It entails making the deliberate decision to stop focusing on what is absent or deficient and instead concentrate on the blessings and plenty that are already a part of our lives. People who practice thankfulness develop an attitude of appreciation, humility, and delight that seeps into every part of their lives.

4. **Regularly expressing gratitude**

In order to develop a grateful mindset, practicing daily appreciation entails introducing brief yet significant rituals into our daily schedule. A deeper sense of thankfulness and joy can be fostered by setting aside time each day to consider and acknowledge the gifts in our

lives, whether through
journaling, meditation, or vocal
expressions of gratitude. People
who practice thankfulness
develop resilience in the face of
adversity and a positive mindset.

5. Discovering Beauty in the Everyday

Experiencing gratitude
encourages us to see the wonder
and beauty in the everyday
events of life. A beautiful sunrise
or a cozy hug from a loved one
are just two examples of the
innumerable instances of grace
and beauty that can be
discovered every day. People
who practice mindfulness and
presence gain the ability to
appreciate these moments and
find happiness in the small joys
of life.

6. Gratitude in Connections

In relationships, gratitude has a
transforming effect that promotes
closeness, connection, and trust.

Gratitude builds relationships
with family members and fosters
reciprocity and appreciation.
People strengthen their bonds
with one another and start a
beneficial circle of love and
gratitude when they recognize
the contributions and generosity
of others.

7. Gratitude amidst Misery

Gratitude is a guiding light that
provides comfort, perspective,
and resilience even when faced
with hardship and obstacles. It is
possible to cultivate thankfulness
in the midst of adversity by
viewing setbacks as chances for
development and education.
People find the strength, courage,
and hope to face life's obstacles
with grace and thankfulness
when they concentrate on the
lessons, benefits, and silver
linings that come with adversity.

8. Joyfully Distributing Acts of Kindness

Having gratitude spreads kindness and charity, which in turn makes the world a happier and more optimistic place. Spreading happiness to others increases the blessings in our lives and promotes a sense of connectivity and compassion, whether through unplanned acts of kindness, volunteer labor, or charitable donations. By giving back, people make the world a happier and more peaceful place.

9. Gratitude as a Mentality Modifier

Being grateful is more than just saying "thank you" once in a while; it's a complete change in attitude and viewpoint. Reframing obstacles as chances, failures as teaching moments, and gifts from God helps people develop an optimism and resilience that transcends all circumstances. Having gratitude changes the way we view and live, allowing us to be happy and fulfilled in every moment, no matter what is going on around us.

10. **The Path of Appreciation**

Gratitude is a lifelong quest for happiness, contentment, and spiritual development. One moment at a time, the road of self-realization, awakening, and transformation takes place. Let us cultivate a profound sense of gratitude for the gift of life itself as we embrace the practice of thankfulness, opening our hearts to the abundance and beauty that surround us and finding delight in the small things in life.
In summary, gratitude is an incredibly potent energy that may change our lives from the inside out. We can discover the secret to true pleasure and contentment by developing an attitude of thankfulness, practicing gratitude every day, and finding joy in the little things in life. Knowing that thankfulness has the capacity to improve both our lives and the lives of others around us, let's

embrace the practice of gratitude
and take time to appreciate the
good things in life, nurture joy,
and show love and kindness
wherever we go.

Pillar 8: Empowerment: Making the Most of Your Assets

Recognizing and embracing
one's innate strengths, skills, and
abilities to take charge of one's
life and attain both personal and
professional fulfillment is the
process of empowerment. We
will examine the meaning,
advantages, and doable tactics of
empowerment in order to help
you realize your full potential
and live a life that is purposeful.

1. **Recognizing Empowerment**

The concept of empowerment is complex and includes elements like agency, autonomy, and self-assurance. Fundamentally, empowerment is accepting oneself, having faith in one's skills, and acting independently to achieve one's ambitions. People who embrace empowerment develop resilience, self-efficacy, and a will to overcome obstacles and bring about positive change in their lives.

2. Advantages of Self-Empowerment

Numerous advantages exist for both professional and personal development when one is empowered. It raises self-esteem, self-awareness, and self-acceptance, empowering people to confidently follow their passions and appreciate their individuality. Furthermore, empowerment encourages a sense of accountability and ownership since it allows people to take ownership of their decisions and deeds, which increases life happiness and fulfillment.

3. Acknowledging Your Advantages

The acknowledgement and appreciation of one's abilities and qualities is essential to empowerment. Examining your experiences, abilities, and attributes that make you happy and fulfilled is a necessary step in determining your strengths. Knowing what your strengths are—whether they be in creativity, leadership, empathy, or problem-solving—allows you to use them to your advantage in order to accomplish your objectives and improve the world.

4. Building Confidence in Oneself

The foundation of empowerment is self-confidence, which inspires people to take risks and fervently pursue their goals. Self-limiting ideas must be contested, failure must be welcomed as a teaching opportunity, and all accomplishments, no matter how tiny, must be celebrated in order to build self-confidence. People who have strong self-esteem take charge of their lives and overcome adversity with resiliency and resolve.

5. Establishing motivating objectives

Aligning your objectives with your values, passions, and strengths is a crucial step in setting empowering goals. Empowering objectives offer a clear path to achievement because they are SMART (specific, measurable, achievable, relevant, and time-bound). People who develop empowering objectives are better able to prioritize their tasks, define their vision, and maintain motivation and focus as they work for both professional and personal fulfillment.

6. Adopting a Growth Mentality

Empowerment requires a growth mentality since it cultivates the attitude that one can learn, develop, and overcome new obstacles. Adopting a growth mindset means seeing obstacles as chances for improvement, asking for and accepting constructive criticism and feedback, and seeing setbacks as stepping stones toward achievement. People who have a growth mindset embrace lifelong learning and development and realize their full potential.

7. Developing Resilience

The capacity to overcome hardship and misfortune with fortitude and grace is known as resilience. Creating social support networks, learning coping mechanisms, and keeping an optimistic attitude in the face of adversity are all part of building resilience. People who have developed resilience are better able to withstand life's ups and downs and come out stronger and more capable than they were before.

8. Looking for guidance and assistance

It is not necessary to travel the path of empowerment alone; getting help and mentoring can hasten development. Building a network of supportive peers, looking for mentorship, and surrounding yourself with positive influences will help you overcome challenges and accomplish your goals. Mentoring others also gives you a sense of purpose and joy because you are sharing your expertise and experience to help others along their journey.

9. Taking Charge and Being Responsible

Taking charge of your life and acting proactively to design the life you want is the essence of empowerment. Taking action entails moving beyond your comfort zone, accepting uncertainty, and grasping chances for personal development and discovery. You may regain control over your life and create the conditions for both professional and personal fulfillment by accepting responsibility for your choices and deeds.

10. Giving Back: Encouraging Others

It's crucial to empower others in return as you embrace empowerment and play to your abilities. Encouraging people to take action, whether through advocacy, mentoring, or community involvement, has a snowball effect on positive change and development. By putting others' needs first, you help create a culture that is more accepting, empowering, and supportive—a place where everyone may prosper.

In summary Acknowledging and using your strengths is the first step on the path to empowerment, which is a journey of self-improvement, growth, and transformation. You may reach your full potential and live a purpose-driven life by developing self-confidence, establishing empowering goals, adopting a growth mindset, and taking proactive measures to bring about positive change. As you make use of your abilities and embrace empowerment, don't forget to give back by empowering others and changing the world for the better.

Pillar 9: Harmony in Life: Establishing Balance

The art of maintaining harmony and sustainability while balancing several facets of life, such as relationships, career, health, and personal development, is known as balance. We examine the importance, advantages, and doable tactics of balance in order to foster harmony in our lives and general well-being.

1. Recognizing Equilibrium

Achieving perfection or allocating the same amount of time and effort to each aspect of life is not what balance is all about. Rather, it entails setting priorities and dividing up resources—time, effort, and focus—in accordance with one's requirements, priorities, and values. Maintaining harmony despite life's swings requires constant assessment, adjustment, and flexibility, as balance is a dynamic and ever-evolving concept.

2. The Advantages of Equilibrium

There are many advantages to achieving balance in life for one's mental, emotional, and physical health. People who are balanced report feeling less stressed, more resilient, and having a higher quality of life overall. Additionally, when people find harmony and resonance in their objectives and interests, balance promotes increased productivity, creativity, and fulfillment.

3. Setting Priorities

The capacity to recognize and order the things that are most important is the foundation of balance. Determining priorities entails considering one's values, objectives, and aspirations and allocating time, effort, and resources appropriately. People make a plan for a balanced life by defining their priorities and concentrating on the things that make them happy, fulfilled, and meaningful.

4. Defining Limits

In order to keep things in balance
and protect one's wellbeing,
boundaries must be set.
Establishing boundaries entails
stating your intentions clearly
and politely to other people.
Setting limits enables people to
safeguard their time, energy, and
mental health, promoting a sense
of balance and autonomy. These
boundaries might be set about
job hours, personal time, or
social obligations.

5. Accepting Self-Care

A key component of balance is
self-care, which includes
activities that nourish and restore
the body, mind, and spirit.
Exercise, a good diet, meditation,
and relaxation techniques are
only a few examples of self-care
activities. However, all of them
emphasize putting one's needs
and well-being first. People who
practice self-care refuel, lower
their stress levels, and build

resilience so they can face life's obstacles with poise and ease.

6. Engaging in mindfulness practices

Being totally present and involved in the here and now, free from distraction or judgment, is the practice of mindfulness. People who practice mindfulness become more conscious of their thoughts, feelings, and bodily sensations, which helps them deal calmly and clearly with life's ups and downs. People who practice mindfulness learn to handle the difficulties of life with greater present and intention, which leads to a sense of balance and inner calm.

7. Developing Adaptability

In the face of the unavoidable changes and difficulties that come with life, flexibility is crucial for preserving equilibrium. Being flexible means accepting ambiguity, adjusting to unanticipated events, and viewing failures as chances to improve. People who practice flexibility manage changes and challenges with grace, resiliency, and agility, preserving balance in the ebb and flow of life.

8. Building Relationships

Maintaining relationships with others is essential to balance because it promotes a feeling of fulfillment, support, and belonging. Social support networks are strengthened, and one's life is enhanced by establishing connections, whether it is through community service, friendships, or spending time with loved ones. People who prioritize connection build deep connections that uplift their spirits and promote general wellbeing.

9. Following your purpose and passion

Finding balance entails directing one's activities and endeavors with enthusiasm and intention. Finding your passion and purpose requires incorporating the things that make you happy and fulfilled into your everyday activities. Aligning oneself with one's passion and purpose gives life meaning, energy, and fulfillment and promotes harmony and balance. This can be achieved through volunteering, engaging in extracurricular activities, or finding meaningful employment.

10. Accepting Your Imperfection

It's critical to accept imperfections and let go of impractical expectations in the quest for balance. Perfectionism undermines one's attempts to attain balance by frequently causing stress, fatigue, and unhappiness. People can let go of the need to appear perfect and accept the complexity of life with grace by accepting imperfection and engaging in self-compassion practices.

In summary, balance is a process that involves constantly changing and adapting to stay in tune with what is most important while promoting overall wellbeing. It is not a destination. People build resilience, fulfillment, and joy, as well as harmony, in their lives by defining priorities, establishing boundaries, taking care of themselves, and establishing connections. Since true harmony arises from connecting with our values, passions, and purpose, let us embrace balance as a way of life and negotiate life's complexity with grace, flexibility, and intention.

Pillar 10: Legacy: Making an Intense Impression Overview

A legacy is our mark on the world, comprised of the

principles we uphold long after
we are gone, the lives we touch,
and the effects we make. This
study delves into the importance
of legacy, its advantages, and
doable tactics for making a
lasting impression that will
benefit present and future
generations.

1. Recognizing Legacy

A legacy is the impression we
make on other people's hearts
and minds, not only our
accomplishments or material
belongings. It's about the
relationships we build, the ideals
we uphold, and the contributions
we make to society as a whole.
The essence of our identity and
the way we are regarded by those
whose lives we have impacted is
our legacy.

2. The importance of tradition

Our lives are given meaning and
purpose by our legacy, which

motivates us to live intentionally
and change the world for the
better. The beliefs and customs
we instill in our future
generations influence their lives,
creating a sense of continuity and
connection that spans
generations. A legacy is a proof
of our existence and a means of
making sure that our influence
endures even after we are gone.

3. **Thinking Back on
    Principles and Ideas**

Reflection on our values, beliefs,
and guiding principles—which
direct our behaviors and
decisions—lays the foundation of
a legacy. Thinking about our
values means deciding what is
most important to us—be it
justice, compassion, honesty, or
creativity—and then acting in a
way that is consistent with those
values. We leave a legacy that
embodies our true selves and
encourages others to follow in
our footsteps when we live
according to ourselves and our
basic values.

4. Developing Bonds

Since one of the most significant components of our legacy is the impact we have on other people's lives, relationships are the foundation of our legacy. Building deep bonds with coworkers, friends, family, and neighbors is a key component of nurturing relationships. We leave a lasting legacy of love and support that improves the lives of people we come into contact with by encouraging understanding, compassion, and respect for one another.

5. Using Service to Make a Difference

Serving others is a potent way to make a difference and advance society. Making a difference through service, whether through advocacy, philanthropy, or volunteer work, leaves a legacy of kindness, generosity, and social responsibility. By tackling urgent social issues and providing support to underprivileged areas, we leave a good legacy of change that elevates humanity and improves the globe.

6. Exchanging insights and understanding

One of the most classic ways to leave a lasting legacy is to share information and insight. Giving information to others through writing, teaching, or mentoring enables them to grow, learn, and prosper. We impart wisdom to future generations by sharing our experiences, perceptions, and lessons learned, which enables them to face life's obstacles with poise and fortitude.

7. Maintaining customs and culture

Since culture and traditions help us stay connected to our history and roots, they are essential parts of our legacy. Stories, rites, and practices that commemorate our common identity and past must be passed down in order to preserve culture and traditions. Respecting our cultural history leaves a legacy of resilience, identity, and belonging that fortifies neighborhoods and encourages intergenerational harmony.

8. Embracing Innovation and Creativity

Innovation and creativity leave a legacy of ingenuity and transformation, acting as catalysts for advancement and change. New ideas, solutions, and opportunities are sparked by stimulating creativity and innovation, whether through the arts, sciences, technology, or business. By exceeding the limits of what is feasible and having the courage to dream large, we leave a legacy of creativity and inspiration that influences future generations.

9. Ecology Prudence

Environmental stewardship is essential to leaving a sustainable legacy for future generations. Living sustainably, preserving natural resources, and safeguarding ecosystems and biodiversity are all part of taking care of the earth. We leave a legacy of environmental responsibility and stewardship that guarantees a healthy planet for future generations by supporting environmental conservation and implementing eco-friendly activities.

10. Leading a genuine and honest life

The most significant legacy we can leave behind is one of honesty and sincerity. Speaking our truth, acting in accordance with our moral principles, and remaining loyal to who we are in the face of difficulty are all parts of living an ethical life. By leading genuine lives, we encourage others to follow suit. Our legacy of integrity, bravery, and authenticity echoes through the ages and motivates coming generations to lead meaningful lives.

In summary, the core of our identity and the difference we make in the world is our legacy. We leave a lasting legacy that enriches future generations by thinking back on our principles, cultivating relationships, changing the world through service, and leading honest and true lives. Remember that every action we take today affects the legacy we leave behind tomorrow as we work to create a legacy of love, compassion, and good change.

Conclusion: Accepting Growth as an Ongoing Process

Life is a journey, an ongoing process of encounters, obstacles, and chances for development and self-discovery. In this last investigation, we consider what it

means to grow as a lifetime
process and the transformative
potential it possesses to mold our
lives and the world around us.

1. Development as a Changing Process

Instead of being a goal, growth is
a dynamic process that takes
place over the course of a
lifetime and involves self-
discovery, learning, and
evolution. It includes aspects that
are mental, emotional, spiritual,
and physical as people work to
improve themselves. Accepting
growth as a continuous process
throughout life entails realizing
that nothing stays the same and
that every experience—no matter
how good or bad—presents a
chance for development and
transformation.

2. The Influence of Mentality

Developing a growth mentality,
or the conviction that aptitude

and intelligence can be enhanced through commitment and work, is fundamental to accepting growth. People with a growth mentality are more able to accept difficulties, keep going after obstacles, and see failures as chances for improvement. People can reach their full potential and start a road of ongoing self-improvement and development by adopting a growth mindset.

3. Acquiring Knowledge from Experience

Experiences in life are priceless teachers on the path to personal development. Every experience, whether it is triumphing over hardship, conquering barriers, or enjoying achievements, brings knowledge and understanding that advances both one's career and personal growth. We develop the resilience and wisdom necessary to handle life's ups and downs with grace and tenacity by thinking back on events, recognizing the lessons they have taught us, and applying them to our daily lives.

4. Accepting Change

On the path of progress, change is unavoidable, and accepting it is crucial for both individual and group development. Letting go of resistance and fear and welcoming change and uncertainty with an open heart and mind are essential components of embracing change. People who embrace change are able to adjust to changing circumstances, investigate novel avenues, and spur advancements both individually and as a society.

5. Developing Resilience

The capacity to overcome hardship and misfortune with fortitude and grace is known as resilience. Building social support networks, creating coping mechanisms, and keeping an optimistic attitude in the face of adversity are all part of cultivating resilience. Through developing resilience, people overcome obstacles in life with resiliency, flexibility, and persistence, becoming stronger and more capable than they were before.

6. Developing Self-Compassion

Since self-compassion is treating oneself with love, understanding, and acceptance—especially during difficult or unsuccessful times—it is a fundamental component of growth. Recognizing one's humanity, accepting one's imperfections, and treating oneself with the same love and support that one would provide to a friend are all necessary for cultivating self-compassion. On the path of development, people can develop resilience, self-worth, and inner peace by engaging in self-compassion practices.

7. Looking for possibilities for growth

Accepting growth as a continuous process throughout life entails looking for chances to learn, explore, and advance personally. The pursuit of formal education, learning new skills, or venturing beyond one's comfort zone are all examples of how looking for growth opportunities broadens perspectives and promotes both professional and personal development. People who embrace fresh experiences and difficulties continue to grow and evolve as they progress.

8. Developing Bonds

Relationships are essential to the growth process because they offer companionship, support, and chances for development. Building deep connections with mentors, coworkers, friends, and family who encourage and assist one's personal development is an important part of nurturing relationships. Through the cultivation of empathy, comprehension, and reciprocal regard, people establish a nurturing community that enhances their existence and expedites their individual growth.

9. Taking Up Genuineness

Since authenticity is living in accordance with one's values, beliefs, and objectives, it is the cornerstone of growth. Adopting authenticity means owning one's truth without reservation and accepting one's individual strengths, eccentricities, and flaws. People who embrace authenticity live life on their own terms, pursuing their passions and purpose with conviction and developing self-awareness, confidence, and fulfillment.

10. Making a Trace

In the end, the path of growth involves not only personal

advancement but also making a constructive contribution to the globe and the next generation. Being a role model, motivating others, and improving the lives of others are all part of leaving a legacy. People who accept growth as a continuous process provide a legacy of fortitude, empathy, and self-determination that endures and improves the world for future generations.

In summary Accepting progress as a continuous process that impacts both our lives and the environment is a life-changing experience. A journey of ongoing self-discovery, learning, and development is what people who adopt a growth mindset do: learn from their experiences, embrace change, and develop resilience and self-compassion. By cultivating connections, pursuing personal development, and embracing genuineness, we leave a legacy of fortitude, empathy, and self-determination that motivates people and enhances the planet for future generations. With bravery, curiosity, and an open heart, let us welcome

growth as a lifelong adventure,
understanding that each step we
take will bring us one step closer
to reaching our greatest potential
and changing the world for the
better.

www.ingramcontent.com/pod-product-compliance
Lightning Source LLC
Chambersburg PA
CBHW051839250726

48659CB00005B/1930